The Whole Hog

odd phrases and idioms explained

To Martha and Jo

THE WHOLE HOG

Odd phrases and idioms explained.

Oliver Dalton and Gray Jolliffe

CORGI BOOKS

Sleeping Like a Top

Sleeping soundly

The other form of this idiom is 'sleeping like a log'; oddly enough both are drawn from the same source.

Crudely made tops are nothing more than a sharpened stick – and for that reason were nicknamed 'log'. When a top is spun very rapidly, the uppermost part will appear to be perfectly still – and is said to be 'sleeping'.

And, by the way, since 'nickname' is mentioned above, you might like to know that it's one of those words formed by the addition of an 'n' when the word 'an' precedes a noun. Sometimes we've lost the 'n' – 'umpire' from 'a numpire', or 'uncle' from 'my uncle' (mine uncle, as it became in the sixteenth century). As often, we've gained the 'n' – 'newt' from 'an ewt' and 'nickname' from 'an ekename', where 'eke' simply means 'other'.

Not many people know that.

Playing to the Gallery

Over-emphasis; trying to appeal to everyone

When the Beatles played the Royal Command Performance, John Lennon asked those in the cheap seats to clap their hands in time with the music; 'Those in the expensive seats', he said, 'can just rattle their jewellery.'

Well, the gallery would have been clapping; it's the least expensive place in the house. Performers whose acts were not going down well would often resort to lowering the tone in the hope of appealing to the people in the cheap seats – the supposition being that they were likely to possess a coarser sense of humour.

It's also been suggested that, because the *very* cheap seats, the top tiers, are called 'the gods', an actor who was having a bad day would 'appeal to the gods'.

It's Touch and Go

A fifty-fifty chance of success or disaster

Since it's difficult to date this idiom, it could have been drawn from chariot racing, trotting or early racetrack driving. It refers to the moment when two vehicles are abreast, each challenging for the lead, and their wheels momentarily clash. Sometimes that spells tragedy; at other times the drivers might be lucky enough to just touch and continue.

4

This is your captain speaking. Many of you will have noticed that the controls have gone haywire and that we are heading for that mountain. There is no need to PANIC!

Haywire

Out of control; behaving in an unruly manner

In modern life, there are some objects that seem to have been designed for awkwardness and uncontrollability: sticky tape, chewing gum (after use), telephone cords, window blinds and so forth. One such is baling-wire, or hay-wire, which is strong, springy and — when it's put under tension just before it goes round the bale — seems to have a life of its own.

He Was Stymied

He was baulked; in a very difficult position

Golf is one of those games that can drive the average player into a frenzy; the whole thing can seem to be a series of frustrating ill luck, and a day on the links can reduce a normally calm man to a cursing wreck.

It's just as well, perhaps, that the rule from which this phrase derives is now obsolete. At one time, if your opponent's ball wound up on the lie between yours and the hole on the putting green it stayed there — no marking was allowed. So, through no fault of your own, you'd be obliged to make a chip on what might have been a two-foot putt. The unfortunate player was said to have been 'laid a stymie'.

Gutter Press

Disreputable newspapers; scandal sheets

Given that the gutter is where filth and refuse flow (especially in earlier days when it was a channel for sewage), you could be excused for thinking that this idiom is self-explanatory.

In fact, it refers to the practice of printing popular literature – newspapers included – with wide margins for easy reading. The double margin where a book or paper folds is known by printers as the gutter.

Nothing But Frippery

Irreverence or silliness

Frippery at one time simply meant something of very little value – the sort of object one might find among the odds and ends in a junk shop.

A fripperer was someone who used to buy and sell second-hand clothes – cast-offs. Because such people often used to travel from town to town with their wares, it was a term sometimes applied to the rag-and-bone men who are still seen from time to time, driving small horse-drawn carts and collecting anything that people are glad to part with.

The Devil to Pay

A serious outcome of some action or another

This might sound straightforward enough, but it's not. In the days of wooden ships, a 'devil' was a seam that ran between the planks forming the lowest part of the stern and the part that actually sat in the water. It was notoriously difficult to get at when the ship was being caulked – that is, when the seams were being treated with tar to keep them waterproof.

The full saying is 'The devil to pay and no pitch hot ' -'pay' being a technical word (rarely in use now) that means to smear with tar.

Running the Gauntlet

Undergoing hardship; attacked from all sides

First of all, the 'gauntlet' in question is not a glove – it's a corruption of 'gantlope', the term given to the space between two rows of men. A common form of punishment for soldiers during the seventeenth century was to make the victim run through the gantlope while those forming the lines – each of them armed with a rope's end – lashed at him as hard as they could. Those who made it were probably first in line when the gantlope was formed for someone else.

Gone to Pot

Suffering ill-fortune

Nowadays you'll find a recipe for stew in most general cookbooks. At one time, though, it was pretty much the last resort for an ordinary family. Unlike the modern stew with its carefully organized ingredients and precise cooking times, it consisted of any leftovers that came to hand, and the stew-pot would be kept on the go for weeks at a time.

Any just-edible food that was no use for other dishes would go to the pot.

He's a Bigwig

He's someone of great importance or influence

The eighteenth century may have been the Age of Reason, but couldn't claim to be the age of hygiene. The streets were full of garbage and, as often as not, people's hair was full of lice. About the only way of dealing with this problem was to cut off the lousy tresses and then — so that one didn't parade the streets looking like a recently released criminal — invest in a wig.

Human vanity being what it is, those of the nobility, people 'in society' and professional types who considered their jobs to be of the first order would sport large and glorious wigs to distinguish themselves from the hoi polloi. The more important the person, the bigger the wig.

9

Utter Havoc

Drastic disorder

Like 'No quarter', this has a military origin. In fact, if no quarter was to be given, havoc (or havok, or havock) was the likely outcome. The first expression meant that no quarters, or accommodation, would be provided for prisoners – largely because there weren't going to be any. Havoc was also an instruction to massacre without mercy. The most famous use of the term is in Shakespeare's *Julius Caesar*: 'Cry havoc, and let slip the dogs of war.'

Sent to Coventry

Made to feel unwelcome; deliberately ignored as a form of punishment

Among those groups who tend not to have a good reputation – soccer fans, Hell's Angels, politicians – are soldiers when they are billeted on some unwilling town. Legend has it that the people of Coventry suffered more than most from having their homes requisitioned for squaddies who were being marched north to quell some rebellion or another. So great was their dislike of the troops that any citizen seen talking to a soldier was likely to become very unpopular with his or her neighbours.

As a result, any soldier posted to Coventry knew that he was not going to get the opportunity to chat to the local lovelies. Indeed, he could count on being greeted everywhere with a stony silence.

Spare the Rod and Spoil the Child

Too much leniency leads to indiscipline

Victorian nannies were much given to this adage, believing that stern measures would result in good behaviour. They took their text from the Bible: 'He that spareth his rod hateth his child. . . .

However, they would have been horrified to learn that the saying had been given an altogether different emphasis by a contemporary poet – a man whose decidedly kinky sexual tastes included a liking for flagellation. In a poem, he urges his mistress to 'spare not the rod nor spoil the child' – the child, in this case, being Cupid.

A Load of Old Cobblers

Nonsense; sometimes, a pack of lies

Cockney rhyming slang was first used as a system of code among members of the East End underworld. A two-word phrase would be found to rhyme with the intended word, then the rhyming word omitted, so that the first word indicated what was being said. So 'trouble' is trouble and strife: wife; 'apples' is apples and pears: stairs; 'butchers' is butcher's hook: look; and 'Khyber' is Khyber pass: arse. So when you know that 'cobblers' is cobbler's awls, it doesn't take too much imagination to work out the rest.

All at Sixes and Sevens

Confused; ill-organized

Americans call it craps, the English call it dicing, but whatever the name, games involving the throwing of dice on a wager have existed for a very long time. In one form of the game, a bet can be made that predicts either a six or a seven as the total count for one throw. Someone who has his money on sixes and sevens would be leaving everything to fortune – and the saying has come to mean something rather like 'everything in the air' rather than its original sense of 'everything at risk'.

In the Doghouse

In disgrace

Yes, you're right – it means just what it says
. . . confined to the kennel. But you might like
to know why.

In J. M. Barrie's play, *Peter Pan*, the man of
the house, Mr Darling, ill-treats Nana the dog,
and believes that to be why his children have
flown away to Never-Never Land. He vows
that, until they return, he'll sleep in Nana's
kennel. It may be that because Nana was a
female dog (the correct term might lead to
misinterpretation) the term has come to be
applied to a man who is out of favour with
his wife.

In Seventh Heaven

Gloriously happy

Getting into heaven, as everyone knows, is not an easy business. Not content with just average difficulty, a society of religious thinkers called cabbalists developed the theory of a system of heavens, each more desirable – and higher – than the last.

The seventh heaven was the abode of God and the best class of angel. No one could imagine a happier place to be.

A Pig in a Poke

Something bought blind; a dubious bargain

It used to be common, at country fairs, for people to buy and sell livestock – a chicken for supper that night, perhaps, or , if you could afford something a bit grander , a sucking pig. It's no surprise that the fairs would be attended by some of the local rogues, who would often take with them a small sack (or poke) with a cat inside it; they would then try to persuade prospective buyers that inside the tightly laced bag was a plump piglet.

To untie the poke and take a look was to run the risk of losing your piglet – they're notoriously fast on their feet. Or you could take the risk and trust the seller.

If someone did happen to open the poke, and discovered that he was being cheated, he would have 'let the cat out of the bag'.

To Rest on Your Laurels

To settle for what you've already achieved; to stop trying

The laurel wreath is still a symbol of victory. It was given that significance by the ancient Greeks, who would award a wreath of wild laurel to the winner of the Olympic Games. It was their belief that the bush possessed the power to bestow on the recipient the gift of prophecy – so maybe he would be able to predict who would win the following year, make a sizeable bet and thereafter rest on his laurels.

Taking French Leave

Going absent without permission; idling

It might be that England's frequent conflicts with France over the years led to a general tendency to identify scandalous or irresponsible behaviour as typically French. To the English, a condom is 'a French letter', venereal disease is 'the French complaint' or 'French gout'. In the same way, the French were characterized as a lazy and shiftless lot, and however untrue that might be the idea gave rise to this idiom.

The French retaliated. To them, to take French leave is *filer à l'anglaise,* while they characterized flagellation – and a few other seamy sexual practices – as *le vice anglais.*

As Right as Ninepence

Precise; correct; some time used to mean 'in good health'

Anyone who's found a pub with a traditional bowling alley, or has bowled for a pig at a village fair, will know that old-style English bowling uses nine pins which have to be carefully replaced, by hand, after each man's turn.

In order to make sure that everyone has the same chance, it's important that the pins are replaced precisely in three rows – that they are set up 'nicely'.

'Ninepence' is a corruption of ninepins. And the original phrase was 'As nice as ninepins' – something that's exactly right.

Eating Humble Pie

Offering an apology; admitting that one was in the wrong

Just as 'ninepins' became 'ninepence', so the original word in this phrase – umbel – became 'humble'. In this case, though, there's a distinct connection between the original word and its replacement.

When kings and nobles used to go hunting for their venison, it would be the huntsmen who did most of the work. But after the beast had been caught, killed and butchered, and the feast was under way, the king and his cronies would enjoy the prime cuts while the huntsmen would have to content themselves with the liver and lights – or 'umbel' as it was called. Not too appetizing a dish; and to make the best of it, the hunt servants would put this offal into a pie.

15

Catch as Catch Can

To perform a task by any means possible

Whether or not wrestling is a 'fix', there are certain rules that have to be observed and certain tactics that will lead to disqualification. For example, there are (and it's just as well) certain parts of the anatomy that shouldn't be grabbed, twisted, pummelled or poked. It wasn't always so. Catch-as-catch-can wrestling permitted the contestants to get a grip on anything, and by any means possible. Eyes could be jabbed, noses yanked, ears rearranged; other possibilities are too horrible to be contemplated.

Beyond the Pale

Outragious behaviour; something or someone wholly unacceptable

It's often been a fault in the English to consider themselves the best judge of what is, and what is not, civilized behaviour, or to consider themselves to be the best representatives of decency and order. In fourteenth-century Ireland, 'The English Pale' was the name given to that part of the country under English rule. 'Pale' derives from 'paling' or fence. Anything beyond the pale was thought to be outside the bounds of polite English society.

You Can Whistle for It

Don't expect to get whatever it is you want

This idiom has changed its meaning somewhat in recent years, It now implies that a request isn't going to be granted or — more aggressively — that a debt won't be paid.

Its earlier meaning was rather more to do with a warning. In the days of sail, there was a common superstition that a wind could be summoned by whistling, though not all becalmed sailors were in favour of the idea. Some believed that whistling was 'the Devil's music' and therefore likely to bring a gale to wreck the ship. 'You can whistle for it' meant 'Take the risk if you dare — you might get more than you bargained for.'

To Take Someone Down a Peg

To deflate a pompous person; to make such a person look small

Under normal circumstances, a ship flies the flag of its country, though on special occasions it will fly all its colours — particularly when its crew is being honoured for some reason or another.

It used to be the case that the colours were raised or lowered by means of a series of pegs.The higher the colours were flown, the greater the honour to the ship and its company; so clearly, if the colours were raised higher than they should have been, orders were given that they should be taken down a peg. Or maybe even two.

You Got Out of Bed the Wrong Side

You are in an ill temper

The left side has always seemed to stand for things sinister, unlucky or just plain bad. We speak of a left-handed compliment, meaning false praise; a bar sinister — the sign of bastardry — on a heraldic shield runs from right to left; the word 'sinister' itself is from a Latin word meaning 'on the left side'.

For similar reasons, it was taken to be a bad omen if someone set his left foot on the floor first when getting up in the morning.

17

Three Sheets in the Wind

Drunk, referring particularly to someone who is unsteady on his feet

Some drunks are noisy and aggressive, others guilty and depressive; but a common characteristic among those who hit the bottle is a tendency to weave, wobble and fall down.

'Three sheets in the wind' is a nautical term. A sheet is a rope used for trimming sail. If it comes loose, the sail will flap about in an ungainly way — and is said to be 'in the wind'. This idiom takes that image of tipsiness and multiplies it by three, indicating someone who's not just drunk, not just pretty drunk, but falling-down drunk.

Watch your Ps and Qs

Be well-mannered and polite

Anyone who has kids will know that when they start to learn to write, they tend to get confused by some letters of the alphabet and form them back to front. You only have to look at p and q to see that they are the two letters most likely to be muddled. By extension, the phrase is a warning to children to pay attention and behave well.

There's another theory, though, that the idiom has to do with the (now dead) practice whereby pub landlords would chalk up what customers had drunk in the course of an evening; the bill would be settled at closing time. A 'P' would indicate a pint; a 'Q' would indicate a quart. So someone 'three sheets in the wind' would have to be careful about what the landlord had put on the slate.

Slapdash

Inferior; done hurriedly

One of the more recent fashions in interior decoration is a process called 'ragging', which involves laying paint on a wall with rags, newspapers or a sponge, rather than a brush, so that an effect is produced that looks startlingly similar to wallpaper. It's an immensely difficult technique and decorators who can do it well are at a premium.

Householders of an earlier age, however, would have been appalled by the idea. Wallpaper was *de rigueur,* and anyone who tried to imitate a wallpaper effect with paint would have been thought 'beyond the pale'. Some poorer people had to opt for this method though, however second-rate it might have seemed. The paint would be applied with what was then called a slap and a dash in order to obtain the required texture and pattern.

Toeing the Line

Behaving correctly; obeying the rules

Anyone who's watched a group of runners jostling and nudging one another as they fight for a good position on the first bend will realize how important it is to have a yard or two's advantage. Before blocks and other modern paraphernalia were invented, runners would simply stand behind a painted line at the start of a race, getting as close to it as possible.

A cheat might try to get his foot over the line in order to be just a fraction ahead when the gun sounded; an honest man would put his toe as close to the line as possible, but not step over it.

The Whole Hog

All the way; without reservation

Monetary systems used to be a good deal simpler than they are today. It used to be possible, for example, to spend a portion of an English shilling by simply breaking off one, two or three parts of the coin, which was deeply scored with two lateral crosses for just that purpose.

The 'tail' side of a shilling bore the image of a pig; so you could be thrifty and part with only a quarter or, in a rash moment, spend the lot — go the whole hog.

Not Worth His Salt

**Said of someone who isn't working
hard enough to justify his pay**

The Latin for salt is *sal*. The *salarium* was a
ration of salt given – together with other
necessities of life – to soldiers in the legions as
part of their wage. Whether or not the soldiers
were happy with this arrangement isn't clear,
though something might be inferred from the
fact that, eventually, hard cash was
substituted. The payment still went by the
same name, though, and eventually became
our 'salary'. Obviously, a lazy man wasn't
worth the salt ration.

It's as simple as that.

Paying Through the Nose

Settling a large debt, often against one's will

The inhabitants of Denmark might well now seem to be a gentle and civilized race; but that wasn't always so. The marauding hordes that landed on the beaches of England and Ireland during the ninth century had some extremely nasty habits – so much so that a common prayer at the time went: 'From the fury of the Danes, O Lord, deliver us.'

The phrase comes from a tax imposed on the Irish by the Danes; it was called the nose tax, since those who failed to pay it found themselves suffering one of the Danes' less than amusing punishments – they would have their nostrils slit.

Swinging the Lead

Idling; avoiding work that one should be doing

Sailors once used to take soundings with a weighted rope, knotted at intervals to let them know the depth of the water. 'Mark one,' would come the first shout, then 'mark twain', which is how the author of *Tom Sawyer* came to choose his *nom de plume*.

It must have been one of the easier shipboard jobs – a lot less arduous than scrubbing decks or taking a turn in the crow's nest, and the longer it lasted, the better the sailor taking soundings would like it. To avoid other work, he might simply lean over the ship's side and swing the lead to and fro for a while.

Knocked Into a Cocked Hat

Defeated

Another idiom from the game of ninepins. When the pins were set up, the innermost three were placed in triangular formation – the same shape as the cocked hat known best, perhaps, for having been worn by every highwayman who ever graced the Hollywood screen.

A strike that downed six pins would be a good one; and when only the three in the centre were left after one bowl, the pins would be said to have been knocked into (the shape of) a cocked hat.

He's Doolally

He's eccentric; slightly crazy

The British colonization of India resulted in (among other more important things) many Indian words being incorporated into the language: bungalow, for example, and wallah.

Doolally is another. Soldiers who had finished serving their time in India, and were about to be sent home, would wait for their ship in a place called Deolali, near Bombay. Days were long, hot and boring; and the combination of these things gave rise, from time to time, to some pretty eccentric behaviour among the weary and frustrated soldiery.

Turning Over a New Leaf

Changing one's behaviour; trying to reform

This notion of starting afresh comes — not surprisingly — from the business of turning to a new page in a book (another chapter, another part of the story), or in a ledger (beginning a new account). Why 'leaf' though? Well, before the invention of paper, the leaves of some plants were used for writing on; and many of the terms that relate to books have to do with that fact. Folio (a double page, or a page folded once) is from the Latin *folius* — a leaf; paper derives from papyrus; and book is from Old English *boc* — a beech tree.

It's new — wanna turn it over?

All My Eye and Betty Martin

Nonsense; false information

Well, no one knows for sure. . . . But the most likeable explanation is that during the First World War English soldiers, who rarely spoke any foreign language, would represent various words phonetically – which is how Ypres became Wipers. The story goes that the troops would often have heard their French counterparts uttering a popular prayer to St Martin (the patron saint of soldiers) which began: *'O mihi, beate Martine.'* Since this would have sounded like gibberish to the Brits, and since their rendition of it was also gibberish, that's what it came to mean.

If it's not true, it deserves to be.

It Got My Dander Up

It made me angry

Like all languages, English is riddled with words that have been taken from other countries, then changed and adapted for local use. The Dutch term *donder* – meaning thunder – was probably imported into America before reaching England, having already been incorporated in this idiom.

There's another theory that suggests the term has to do with the way dander – or scurf – comes to the surface of a horse's coat when the animal is being groomed. It's not a pleasant experience to be enveloped in a cloud of rank dandruff, which is why stable boys whistle – to avoid inhaling the stuff!

NATIONAL DANDER-UP WEEK

To Come a Cropper

To take a fall; to fail

Here's another case of verbal overkill. In essence, neck and crop are pretty much the same thing, except that the neck generally means the part of the body between the head and the shoulders, while the crop is another word for throat. It has come to mean something like 'from head to toe' — all-inclusive; but it stems from the fact that a rider who was thrown from his horse would often land head first — both neck and crop taking the impact.

Payment on the Nail

When no credit is given; immediate payment

A variation on this phrase is 'cash on the nail' — which exactly describes the method of payment in question. In medieval times, after a transaction of some sort had been conducted, payment would be made by placing the money in a shallow dish mounted on top of a post. Viewed from a little way off, the contraption — post and cup — had the appearance of an enormous nail.

Another version of this sort of prompt payment is expressed by the phrase 'cash on the barrelhead'. In later times, an upturned barrel would become a makeshift counter.

Turning the Tables

To gain the upper hand from a losing position

The least likely explanation of this term is that it has to do with a trick pulled by fake spiritualists to impress the gullible. During a seance, a mechanical device would cause the table around which the participants sat to revolve — convincing them that they'd been visited by a spirit presence.

The most frequently quoted source suggests that it was an extravagant ruse in cards. Some say that the man with a losing hand would turn the table to bring another man's cards before him. Not very likely. To begin with, who could believe that no one would notice; and what's more, the person who turned the table might well wind up with a worse hand than before. Most probably it simply referred to the business of pretending to up-end the table accidentally, spilling all the cards and forcing a re-deal.

Spinning a Yarn

Telling a tale – often an untrue one

Again, there are two explanations for this saying, but they differ very little.

One tells us that when sailors were not swinging the lead, they might be performing another routine task – that of mending nets. They would sit on deck, tying and knotting, and tell each other stories to while away the time; and each would try to outdo the other with the extravagance of his tale.

The second version has just the same thing happening between weavers – usually crofters who were part of a cottage industry. Their looms would be set head to head, and the stories, like the shuttles, would go to and fro.

A Lot of Codswallop

Rubbish; useless information; sometimes, lies

Traditional beer drawn straight from the cask was an altogether stronger brew than the brands on sale in most bars nowadays. Likewise, the first bottled beers were a heady drink – except, that is, for a tipple brewed, bottled and marketed at about the turn of the century by a man named Hiram Codd. It was thin stuff and didn't meet with much approval from those in the know. 'Wallop' has for a long time been an English slang term for beer; and it was well known at the time that Codd's wallop was barely worth drinking.

In time, the term became a general name for anything inferior.

A Backhander

A bribe

The meaning here has broadened. It still means advantaging oneself, though now it also means giving someone money in order to gain a favour. Its origin is more directly selfish.

An odd ritual still exists which dictates that at a formal dinner the port decanter is passed from hand to hand in a clockwise direction. A drinker at a large dinner party might have to wait some time before the booze got round to him again after he'd poured his first tipple; so those prepared to defy tradition would take back the decanter in order to bring another glassful 'to hand'.

Redneck

A hick; often used to mean unsophisticated or prejudiced

It seems unfair that this expression should be most often used as a term of abuse, because it originally meant nothing more sinister than a manual labourer, or someone who worked on the land. One of the most common garments worn by such people – cowboys, loggers, farm hands – was a neckerchief, often a red one. Since these people were involved in hard physical work, they'd sweat; and the red dye that would stain their necks marked them out as country boys rather than city slickers.

By a Long Chalk

By a good margin; a large difference

There are two common versions of this idiom: one positive, one negative. 'I beat him by a long chalk', and 'not by a long chalk' – meaning, 'It's impossible.' The origin lies in the practice – especially in schools – of scoring a competition by making a vertical chalk-mark on a blackboard to indicate one point scored. Afer four marks had been made, a fifth would be drawn through them diagonally from bottom to top, and the scores easily counted in groups of five. When the contest ended, the person or group with the longest chalking had won.

Pie in the Sky

An empty promise; something that may or may not be achieved

The squire, the parson and the schoolteacher were once the self-elected guardians of 'proper' behaviour in rural England. The schoolteacher would urge his pupils to 'know their station in life'; the squire would punish them if they didn't toe the line; and the parson would offer them the compensation of a life of ecstasy in heaven if they remained satisfied with their humble lot on earth.

Not everyone believed this; in fact it's true to say that most would have settled for a good time on earth in exchange for promises about the afterlife. One such was a poet, who expressed that idea in these lines:

Work and pray
Live on hay
You'll get pie
In the sky
When you die.

30

Don't tell me – petard trouble?

Hoist with His Own Petard

To become the victim of one's own evil schemes

This is a medieval version of shooting oneself in the foot; or of scoring an own goal, maybe.

A petard was a piece of siege machinery – something akin to a vast barrel without the rest of the gun. It was filled with gunpowder and then fixed to a gate, a barricade or whatever fortification that stood in the way of an advancing army. The officer in charge would then light the gunpowder trail and, if possible, retire. Unfortunately, it wasn't always possible. The petard was a notoriously unstable weapon and much given to exploding before the unhappy officer could get clear. Up would go the petard, the barricade . . . and the luckless man with the torch.

Below the Salt
Inferior; socially unacceptable

The class war may have cooled off a little nowadays, but there was a time when social standing was very closely observed – and indicated in all sorts of complicated and petty ways.

It's still the case that at some formal dinners those sitting at the high table, or top table, are the VIPs – and so it was in the days when vast flagged halls were lit by tapers and banqueting tables groaned under the weight of food. At the centre of the table would be the salt cellar – a massive silver container decorated with ornate designs. To make the social distinctions clear, persons of note sat above the salt (between the salt cellar and the head of the table) and inferior types sat below.

Jerry-built
Poorly (and cheaply) constructed

If a sailing ship met a bad storm while at sea, it was more than likely that some damage would be done to it. After the storm had passed, the crew would have to set to and effect whatever repairs they could by whatever means possible – often using makeshift materials.

The term given to a mast, or rigging, patched up in this way was 'jury' – a jury mast, or jury-rigging. 'Jerry' is a corruption of that word.

Because the term is often applied to a badly built house, there's a suggestion that it derives from what a bombed house looked like after a Jerry (German) raid; but the phrase long pre-dates the Second World War.

Spoiling the Ship for a Ha'porth of Tar
Ruining the effect of something by making a niggardly saving

There are two schools of thought concerning this saying. One is that its origin has to do with the caulking of ships' plankings with tar – if you economize on that, then the whole vessel might be lost.

The other suggests that 'ship' is the local pronunciation of 'sheep' in the English Midlands, and that the term refers to the practice of daubing sheep with tar to protect them against certain illnesses.

Since the second definition is the least convincing (or least logical, perhaps), it's probably the true one.

Straw Poll
Taking public opinion on a certain issue

There are now so many sophisticated methods of polling opinion that it almost seems unnecessary for people to cast a vote at all – the pollsters decide, long before election day, who is going to be the victor.

It's very unlikely that Gallup, MORI and the rest would want to make use of the method of prediction from which this phrase derives. Before computers were able to tell us what we're going to do, sages, prophets and seers would tell the future by casting a handful of straw into the air, then making their judgements according to which way – and how far – the wind took it.

Off the Cuff

Spontaneously; without preparation

It might be said that there's a degree of fakery in this notion.

Actors who tended to forget their lines, and after-dinner speakers who wanted to avoid embarrassing pauses while they tried to remember what to say next, would jot down on their shirt cuffs key lines or words. If in trouble, they'd shoot their cuffs and take a peek. So the phrase didn't quite have to do with the wit and inventiveness that it's come to represent.

There's no record of how forgetful women coped with the problem.

Sowing Wild Oats

Acting irresponsibly, especially in sexual matters

Why 'oats'? Who knows — it could as easily have been barley or rye, since the inference in this phrase is that wild grain is known to be inferior to cultivated grain. More than that, though, wild grain — which grows between the furrows and along the hedgerows — isn't supposed to be there. The clear implication is that, in sowing wild oats, one is doing something that goes beyond the bounds of acceptable behaviour and which might well produce unwanted results.

Stealing the Limelight

Pushing oneself forward; taking attention away from another

Before electricity made it possible for theatres to employ the complicated lighting systems they have today, limelight was the only method of picking out an individual actor in the way that a spotlight can. It was a particularly strong light – the result of a combustion of gases on a pan of lime – and shed a narrow beam.

An ambitious actor – jealous, perhaps, of another's fame – would sometimes step into the limelight and prevent it from reaching the star of the show. There's no record of how many bit-part players were pushed into the orchestra pit as a result.

Tell It to the Marines

**Tell that story to someone more likely
to believe it**

This expression has acquired distinctly cynical
overtones, though it used to mean something
more like 'See if you can convince me by
getting corroborative evidence.'

It is related that Samuel Pepys was once
repeating a story he'd heard from some
sailors; they'd told him that on their voyages
they had seen fish that could fly. Those
listening to Pepys howled with laughter, until
an officer in the Marines, who happened to be
there, confirmed that such creatures existed.
Someone present then remarked that in
future, before an outlandish story was
dismissed as rubbish it should be told to the
Marines, to see whether they might not be
able to confirm it.

As Pleased as Punch

**Delighted — particularly at the
outcome of some venture**

Punch is, of course, the hook-nosed villain of
the children's puppet show, so the origin of
the phrase seems obvious enough. There's a
slightly sinister undertone to it, though, that
has faded with the years. Punch would clout
Judy with his club — and laugh. He'd throw
the baby out of the window — and laugh. He'd
trick the hangman — who'd been sent to
punish him — into hanging himself; and he'd
laugh. So the particular implication of
someone being as pleased as Punch was that
such a person had been successful in some
evil scheme.

A Cock and Bull Story

An unlikely tale; more strongly — a pack of lies

When people used to travel by stagecoach, journeys were long, tiring and often boring. Just as Chaucer's pilgrims told each other tales to pass the time, so travellers on coaches would swap stories to entertain one another.

Often, parties from different coaches, taking different routes, would meet at some staging post when horses were being changed. One stopover involved the London-bound coach pausing for a while at a pub called the Cock, while the coach for Manchester put in at the Bull Inn nearby. Passengers from the Cock and those from the Bull would get together and swap jokes and tales while they waited.

As Mad as a Hatter

Insane; or, at least, very eccentric

The most famous use of this term was by Lewis Carroll in *Alice in Wonderland*. Carroll, however, didn't invent it.

Before modern methods were introduced, the felt from which hats are made was treated and fashioned by hand. Part of the process involved the use of a substance called mercurous nitrate — a mercury compound — and this, in turn, had a pretty devastating effect on the hatters who used it. Their eyes would smart, their limbs would shake, and in addition to that the chemical possessed mood-altering properties that resulted in extreme ill-temper.

It's reported that one hatter — a Buckinghamshire man — grew so eccentric that he gave away everything he owned and lived on grass.

No Man's Land

A place of danger; figuratively, an exposed position

You'd guess right if you supposed that this idiom makes reference to the area between the trenches during the First World War — the muddy expanse that men found themselves in when they went 'over the top', leaving the trenches to try to gain ground, or capture the enemy's position. Once out there, you stood a good chance of being shelled or machine-gunned or both.

Less known is the usage that pre-dates the First World War. When the open field system of farming was common in England, the parcels of land between one man's property and another's were, literally, no man's land, and could be farmed by anyone who chose to; so the term wasn't always a threatening one.

It means what it says, buster, so watch it.

NO, MAN'S LAND

To Fly Off the Handle

To lose one's temper

One of the routine tasks for a blacksmith was
to soak his hammers in water from time to
time, so that the hafts would swell and wedge
themselves more tightly into the hammer-
head. Forgetting to do this could be a serious
business. If the head happened to be loose
when the smith raised it on the backswing,
then the head could, literally, fly off the
handle — causing a good deal of grief to
anyone who happened to be standing in
the way.

1. Fly on the handle

2. Fly off the handle

Wild Goose Chase

A pointless undertaking

This one poses something of a problem. There's no doubt that it refers, quite simply, to the fact that wild geese are notoriously timid and will take flight at the slightest prompting. However, since the only likely means of catching a goose is to shoot it, or net it, it's difficult to imagine why anyone should have thought that anything might be gained by *chasing* it.

To Foot the Bill

To bear the expense of something; to settle an account

The advent of credit cards has made this phrase more appropriate now than it was a few years ago. It comes from a practice once more common among the rich than among those who would most often pay with cash. The well-to-do often kept accounts with tradesmen or restaurants, and would simply sign their names at the foot of each bill until the time came to pay in full.

To Haul Someone Over the Coals

To reprimand severely

Although tax evasion is something of a national sport, those who get caught can find themselves taking a short walk to a long prison sentence, as Al Capone discovered.

There was a time, though, when the punishment was a trifle more severe. Kings were given to raising taxes for wars, or to build palaces, or just because they happened to be short of cash. One of the penalties for those who were reluctant to pay up was to be very slowly drawn across a bed of live coals.

There's another idiom drawn from this unamusing practice, also used to mean remonstrating with someone — ' to give him a roasting'. Think of it next time your tax return arrives.

A Flash in the Pan

A short-lived success

Priming and firing a flintlock rifle was a tiresome and sometimes risky business. The ball would be inserted, then some wadding rammed home; finally a small charge of powder would be dribbled into a cavity beneath the flint. This cavity was called the lock-pan. When the trigger was pulled and a spark struck from the flint, the powder would ignite and set off the charge that propelled the ball . . . . Except that this didn't invariably happen. Sometimes the powder ignited to no effect — and there would simply be a flash in the pan and no shot fired.

Hue and Cry

A pursuit; an investigation

During a fox hunt, horns and yells are used to let the huntsmen and the field know what's going on. A certain call on the horn, or a traditional cry like 'Gone to earth', will tell everyone that the fox is in flight or has found cover.

At one time, criminals were hunted in just the same way. Men were said to be pursued 'with horn and voice'. In this case, the term really means 'cry and cry', since 'hue' comes from a now obsolete French word *huer,* meaning to shout.

Crying Wolf

Warning of danger when none exists

This idiom is drawn from the folk tale in which
a boy is guarding sheep on a hill. For
amusement's sake, he runs into the villages
shouting: 'Wolf, wolf!' The men of the village
snatch up their weapons and set off to kill the
creature; of course, they can't find it. The boy
is so delighted with his prank that he does it
again; then again; until, finally, when a wolf
does appear, no one takes any notice. And the
wolf kills the boy.

It's interesting that there are independent
versions of this story in many countries
throughout the world.

A Scapegoat

Someone who is blamed — or takes the blame — for someone else's wrongdoing

There's a long tradition of rituals that involve off-loading sin on to dumb animals of one species or another. It doesn't seem very fair, but if the sins are great enough then any chance is better than none.

During the Jewish Day of Atonement it used to be the practice to lead two goats to the tabernacle; here one would be dedicated to God, the other to the Devil. God's goat would then be sacrificed; the Devil's would be said to have taken on all the sins of those present. It would then be taken to a lonely place and set free.

If you think about it, you might come to the conclusion that the goat laden with sin got the better deal.

Raining Cats and Dogs

A downpour

This idiom seems to delight children who, presumably, conjure up an image of animals hurtling from the sky and thudding into the pavements.

There's a belief in folklore that the behaviour of cats foretells the weather — a cat in a jumpy or restless mood means rain. It's also a belief that dogs are able to summon a strong wind (possibly because the Norse storm god was attended by wolves). So the cats signify rain, while the dogs represent the violent winds that bring torrential weather.

Pass the Buck

Refuse to take responsibility for some mishap

Two essential attributes in a poker player are
the ability to bluff and a sharp mind. That
being the case, it's difficult to understand why
it might be necessary for players to have to
remind one another whose deal it is.
Nevertheless, the 'buck' was a token of some
kind (possibly a piece of buckshot: hence the
word) that was passed to a player when it was
his turn to take the deal.

Kiss It Better

A symbolic gesture to do with relieving pain

This is one of those intriguing idioms that seem to have nothing oblique about them at all. Surely by kissing the place that's causing the pain – a grazed knee, or a bumped head – one is simply displaying affection and commiseration.

In fact, the gesture once had a much more practical application; and, less commonly, a holy one. It's a leftover from the practice of sucking poison from an infected place – particularly from a snake-bite. Its more miraculous aspect is drawn from the apparently endless number of saints, holy men and damn fools who would kiss lepers to heal them of their affliction.

Down in the Dumps

Low in spirits; depressed

'The pits', as most people know, is a
contraction of 'armpits', though one might be
forgiven for thinking that it meant some
metaphorical hole in the ground that
represented lowness and therefore
depression. So with 'the dumps'. It would be
perfectly logical to suppose that this had
something to do with waste dumps, refuse,
misery and the end of things in general. Not
so. 'The dumps' was the name given, in
Elizabethan times, to any slow, melancholy,
mournful piece of music.

Put Your Foot in It

To blunder; to make an embarrassing error

You might be led to think that the origin of this phrase has to do with the fact that, throughout the ages, animals have been less than careful about where they leave their droppings, and that, throughout the ages, the unwary have trodden, paused, looked and said 'Urgh!' And, in fact, you would be absolutely right.

You might also consider that, throughout the ages, the problem has involved some creatures much larger than dogs. Sheep, cows and goats once wandered through city streets. And before that, there were dinosaurs. . . .

Dressed Up to the Nines

Dressed in extravagantly expensive and fashionable clothes

Another idiom – 'up to the eyes in it' – meaning almost overcome by something, or deeply involved, makes use of the same image, though without the corruption of the word 'eyes'.

'Up to the nines' simply means up to the eyes, or from head to foot; the notion being that the person referred to has put on all his or her finery . . . and maybe overdone things a little. Nines is a vulgarization of the Middle English word for eyes – *eyen*.

She Set Her Cap at Him

To attempt to attract someone; to flirt

Hats go in and out of fashion – except for members of the Royal Family. There was a time, though, when women wore hats on pretty much all occasions – or rather, caps: creations that had a soft headpiece and a stiff brim, often decorated with lace. Some were for everyday wear, some for high days and holidays.

If a lady wanted to look her best in order to make a gentleman notice her, she'd wear her most attractive hat – would set her cap at him.

Suggestions that this idiom has anything to do with modern methods of contraception are entirely untrue.

Kick the Bucket

To die

One explanation of this idiom is that suicides would stand on a bucket, having fixed a noose round their necks, then kick the bucket away. No one has ever explained why a bucket should have been so popular among the depressed and desperate.

A more likely reference is to the 'bucket' or kitchen beam from which the carcass of a pig or lamb used to be suspended before it was butchered – a suitably macabre image for sure, and a fitting one, since the creature would be hung by the heels.

A Pot-boiler

A task performed solely for the reward it brings

Authors writing pulp do it; actors in commercials do it; in fact anyone doing a quick job for quick cash is doing it. The reference, of course, is to the pot that would hang over the fire in poor homes. The communal meal would be cooked there – and any cash was welcome that would provide fuel to keep it boiling and food to put into it.

Looks to me like one of your potboilers Strumpfenberg.

GENTS TAILORS.

Sold Down the River

Betrayed; cheated in some deal or other

Another, slightly less common, version is 'Sent up the river'; both are of American origin, and in each case the river was definitely one of no return.

Down river was the direction taken by boats ferrying slaves who had been sold by owners who considered them no longer fit for domestic work. They were going to a much tougher life working for plantation owners further down the Mississippi.

Up river – up the Hudson in fact – lay the notorious New York prison Sing Sing. Convicts headed in that direction didn't expect to be taking a river trip again for quite some time.

Cock-a-Hoop

Delighted; triumphant

Despite obvious images of cocks crowing on dungheaps while the hens stand round, or cocks on weathervanes encircled by the points of the compass and, indeed, other less polite images, the cock in question here is the bung, or spigot, from a beer barrel.

It's an image something akin to throwing away the cork after a bottle of wine has been opened, signalling one's intention to drink it all. When the cock was drawn and laid atop the iron hoop that bound the stoutest part of the barrel, air was admitted and the beer could flow.

By Hook or by Crook

By any means available – fair or foul

It was long the practice for landowners, lords of the manor and the like to offer the occasional sop to their tenants and workers – a means of helping to keep the lower orders sweet, perhaps, so that they could be kept in their place, pay their tithes and generally respect their betters.

The term 'dole' – unemployment benefit – is drawn from the strips of land between patches of ploughland which were, from time to time, awarded to some peasant farmer by his lord.

'By hook or by crook' refers to the fact that farm tenants were permitted to cut as much firewood as they could drag down with a shepherd's crook and hack off with a billhook.

Donkey's Years

An extremely long time

This is one of those irritating idioms that depends on its own undeniable, but entirely cranky, logic. It refers to the fact that one never sees a dead donkey. So the saying might well be expanded to something like: 'It won't happen until I see a dead donkey.' Why a donkey was selected as the rare corpse — rather than an aardvark, a wart-hog or a lesser-spotted tree-creeper for instance — is another matter.

I'll Mark Your Card for You

I'll explain the truth about matters

This is a horse- or dog-racing expression. The race card provides a list of runners together with their form, numbers, colours and so forth. If you happen to be lucky enough to go racing with someone who knows a lot about the sport or, even better, has managed to get a few hot tips, he might offer to share his knowledge with you by making a tick, or some mark, on your race card against the name of each runner he expects to win.

He Was Laughing Up His Sleeve

Deceiving someone, and taking pleasure in it

Those who find it difficult to lie for gain, look the victim in the eye and keep a straight face would have benefited from the extravagantly large sleeves that adorned Elizabethan clothes. So voluminous were they that it was possible to hide one's face behind them in order momentarily to conceal one's true expression.

Clearly ad men and politicians would have had no use for such a device.

Complete Bedlam

A riot; noisy and robust behaviour

'Bedlam' is a contraction of Bethlehem. St Mary of Bethlehem was a priory which once stood near Bishopsgate in London; in the fourteenth century it became a refuge for the insane. In those days the mad were, by and large, left to fend for themselves – no treatments were available and little was known about lunacy.

How did people know that Bedlam was like – well – bedlam? For a small charge, the public were allowed to go to the priory and stare at the inmates as if they were animals in a zoo. All too often, the spectators would take the opportunity to jeer at the lunatics and torment them.

Stealing Someone's Thunder

To go one better; to divert attention to oneself

John Dennis was a critic and playwright who died in the middle of the eighteenth century. He'd written a play which called for several loud and impressive rolls of thunder. Since he didn't trust the stage management to produce the tumultuous effect he wanted, he invented his own method — rolling cannon balls along the wooden roof of the theatre. It was a great success. Dennis's play, though, wasn't. It closed with ignominious speed.

Not long afterwards, Dennis was at a performance of *Macbeth*, at the same theatre. During the witches' first scene, a great roll of thunder was heard — startlingly effective, and produced by Dennis's own method.

Dennis leaped to his feet. 'God!' he exclaimed, 'they've stolen my thunder.' Clearly the remark was sufficiently memorable to pass into the language.

In a Brown Study

In melancholy or reflective mood

If at any time you happen to see a Frenchman, head in hands, a mournful expression on his face and a vacant look in his eye, you're looking at a man sunk in *sombre rêverie*. Since both *sombre* and *brun* are used by the French to indicate melancholia, whoever thought to translate the phrase picked the more obscure *brun* — and gave us 'brown study'. Maybe he was a depressed interior decorator . . .

To Come Up to Scratch

To perform as required; to acquit oneself well

Before the rumble in the jungle came the hammerings on the heath — or, perhaps, the pastings in the park — where bare-knuckle fighters would meet at some open-air venue to slug it out, while the crowd laid bets on the outcome.

When one of the fighters had been knocked down he was given ten seconds (hence the modern count of ten) to get up and go back to a line scratched across the centre of the roped-off patch where the fight took place.

Cock of the Walk

Someone of importance — often a braggart or bully

This term was often applied to a fighting cock which had an impressive number of victories to its credit, though its origin lies in the humbler surroundings of the barnyard.

When barn fowls were fed, the person throwing the grain would go up and down on a board, or plank, laid from one end of the barn to the other — presumably to keep out of the mud. The grain that fell on the board would be more easily available than that in the mud, and the cockerels would fight for this scrap of territory.

The fifth column? That's value added tax on my commission

Fifth Column

Usually a 'fifth columnist' — someone who is working to undermine one's efforts

Like John Dennis's protest that 'They've stolen my thunder', this idiom passed into the language only because someone who heard it said was sufficiently impressed to make use of it at some other time, and in a way that separated it from its original — and very particular — meaning.

It's a recent addition — dating from the Spanish Civil War. A general who was advancing on Madrid had been sufficiently clever to send ahead a group of men who entered the city in civilian clothes, then set about committing acts of sabotage to make the general's eventual attack an easier matter. 'I have four columns advancing on Madrid', the general was heard to say, 'and a fifth column already in the city.'

Blue Blooded

Noble; of aristocratic origin

If you cut a member of the upper classes (remember to get permission first) you'll discover, of course, that his blood is as red as that of the commonest common man.

Veins, however, do appear blue beneath the skin; and it's a simple verbal short-cut to describing the blood within them as blue . . . or bluer . . . or bluest. *Very* blue blood would mark out those of good breeding, because their pale, smooth skin would show the vein to better advantage than would the hairy, work-roughened skin of the lower orders. That, in any case, is the theory. . . .

The Apple of His Eye

Someone much in favour

It used to be believed that the pupil of the eye
was a solid sphere — round, like an apple. The
fancy that lies behind this idiom is that
someone who was cherished — and therefore
looked at often, and fondly — was held, just as
his reflection would be, in the apple of the
beholder's eye.

Before You Can Say Jack Robinson

Quickly; in no time at all

One theory has it that a gentleman of this name was a well-known eccentric, who would set out to visit a friend, forget who it was he'd intended to see, and go from household to household, leaving each place quickly when he realized that he'd got the wrong man.

A rather more serious version tells of an incident in the House of Commons in the eighteenth century, when an eminent politician was suggesting that there was corruption in the government. Asked to back his allegation by naming names, he looked at an MP called John Robinson and said, 'I could give one instance as soon as say Jack Robinson.'

Above Board

Honest; with nothing to hide

Strangely, this is another idiom which could be drawn from either spiritualism or gambling (as in 'Turn the tables'). The idea was that a fake medium could produce all sorts of startling effects by manipulating apparatus under the table. Or that a gambler whose hands were not above the table could be slipping an ace out of his sleeve.

On Tenterhooks

Apprehensive; anxious about the outcome of some venture

This is often misrepresented as 'on tenderhooks' — the result, probably, of the original word being misheard. However, anyone literally on tenterhooks would certainly feel pretty tender during and after the event.

It's derived from the weaving trade. Newly woven cloth would be tentered — or stretched — on hooks before being baled; so the image of something (or someone) being made tense is what makes the phrase appropriate. It's also where we get the word 'tent' from — something made from stretched canvas.

Win Hands Down

To win effortlessly

Keen punters will have seen this happen many times. In a close finish, with nothing much to choose between the horses as they near the post, the contending jockeys will probably be using their whips — or, at the very least of it, be urging their mounts on by keeping them on a tight rein and kicking with their heels.

A jockey whose horse is winning by several lengths need do none of this. He can afford to slacken rein — ride with his hands down — as he brings his horse home.

Bury the Hatchet

Make peace; settle differences

The derivation of this phrase is precise and direct. It means exactly what it says. When North American Indians smoked a pipe of peace — otherwise called the calumet — they would emphasize their peaceful intentions by burying their weapons of war: clubs, bows, scalping knives and, not least, hatchets.

It might have been a symbolic gesture, but it seems a pretty drastic one. If they were attacked at some later date they would, presumably, have to dig the lot up again.

Pin Money

A small sum; enough to buy small items with

A few centuries ago the roles of the sexes were very clear-cut indeed. You wouldn't have found a man darning his own hose, or putting a tuck in his doublet. There might have been more to this than pointless male pride – pins were ruinously expensive; in fact there are examples of wills being drawn up which made special bequests to people for the purchase of pins.

This aside, women were given set sums of money with which to run the household, but an additional sum specifically for the buying of pins. For this reason, the term came to mean a small, but personal, allowance.

A CORGI BOOK 0 552 993018

Designed and produced by Genesis Productions Limited,
30 Great Portland Street, London W1N 5AD

First publication in Great Britain 1987

This book is set in Egyptian 505 Roman

Corgi Books are published by Transworld Publishers Ltd,
61–63 Uxbridge Road, Ealing, London W5 5SA, in Australia
by Transworld Publishers (Australia) Pty Ltd, 15–23 Helles
Avenue, Moorebank, NSW 2170, and in New Zealand by
Transworld Publishers (NZ) Ltd, Cnr Moselle and
Waipareira Avenues, Henderson, Auckland.

Made and printed in Spain by Mateu Cromo, Madrid